Allen Ginsberg

# THE GATES OF WRATH
*Rhymed Poems: 1948-1952*

Grey Fox Press
Bolinas: 1972

Grateful acknowledgment is made to the following which first pub-
lished some of these poems: *Columbia Review, Gay Sunshine,
Gemini, Metronome, Neurotica, The New American Poetry 1945-
1960, Pull My Daisy,* and *The Raven.*

"A Prefatory Letter" from Williams Carlos Williams, *Paterson,*
Book IV. Copyright 1951 by William Carlos Williams. Reprinted by
permission of New Directions Publishing Corporation.

Cover photograph by the poet in March 1949.

ISBN: 0-912516-01-1

Library of Congress Catalog Card No.: 72-76541

Manufactured in the United States of America

First Edition

Grey Fox Books are distributed by Book People,
2940 Seventh Street, Berkeley, California 94710

To find the Western path
Right thro' the Gates of Wrath
I urge my way;
Sweet Mercy leads me on:
With soft repentant moan
I see the break of day.

WM. BLAKE 1793

This is the one and only
firmament: therefore
it is the absolute world.
There is no other world.
I am living in Eternity.
The ways of this world
are the ways of Heaven.

A. GINSBERG 1950

Thus is the heaven a vortex pass'd already, and the earth
A vortex not yet pass'd by the traveller thro' Eternity.

WILLIAM BLAKE

The yearning infinite recoils,
For terrible is earth!

HERMAN MELVILLE

## Contents

# A PREFATORY LETTER

ALLEN GINSBERG TO WILLIAM CARLOS WILLIAMS

? Month 1949

Dear Doctor:

In spite of the grey secrecy of time and my own self-shuttering doubts in these youthful rainy days, I would like to make my presence in Paterson known to you, and I hope you will welcome this from me, an unknown young poet, to you, an unknown old poet, who live in the same rusty county of the world. Not only do I inscribe this missive somewhat in the style of those courteous sages of yore who recognized one another across the generations as brotherly children of the muses (whose names they well know) but also as fellow citizenly Chinamen of the same province, whose gastanks, junkyards, fens of the alley, millways, funeral parlors, river-visions—aye! the falls itself—are images white-woven in their very beards.

I went to see you once briefly two years ago (when I was 21), to interview you for a local newspaper. I wrote the story in fine and simple style, but it was hacked and changed and came out the next week as a labored joke at your expense which I assume you did not get to see. You invited me politely to return, but I did not, as I had nothing to talk about except images of cloudy light, and was not able to speak to you in your own or my own concrete terms. Which failing still hangs with me to a lesser extent, yet I feel ready to approach you once more.

As to my history: I went to Columbia on and off since 1943, working and travelling around the country and aboard ships when I was not in school, studying English. I won a few poetry prizes there and edited the Columbia Review. I liked Van Doren most there. I worked later on the Associated Press as a copyboy, and spent most of the last year in a mental hospital; and now I am back in Paterson which is home for the first time in seven years. What I'll do there I don't know yet—my first move was to try and get a job on one of the newspapers here and in Passaic, but that hasn't been successful yet.

My literary liking is Melville in Pierre and the Confidence Man, and in my own generation, one Jack Kerouac whose first book came out this year.

I do not know if you will like my poetry or not—that is, how far your own inventive persistence excludes less independent or youthful attempts to perfect, renew, transfigure, and make contemporarily real an old style of lyric machinery, which I use to record the struggle with imagination of the clouds, with which I have been concerned. I enclose a few samples of my best writing. All that I have done has a program, consciously or not, running on from phase to phase, from the beginnings of emotional breakdown, to momentary raindrops from the clouds become corporeal, to a renewal of human objectivity which I take to be ultimately identical with no ideas but in things. But this last development I have yet to turn into poetic reality. I envision for myself some kind of new speech—different at least from what I have been writing down—in that it has to be clear statement of fact about misery (and not misery itself) , and splendor if there is any out of the subjective wanderings through Paterson. This place is as I say my natural habitat by memory, and I am not following in your traces to be poetic: though I know you will be pleased to realize that at least one actual citizen of your community has inherited your experience in his struggle to love and know his own world-city, through your work, which is an accomplishment you almost cannot have hoped to achieve. It is misery I see (like a tide out of my own fantasy) but mainly the splendor which I carry within me and which all free men do. But harking back to a few sentences previous, I may need a new measure myself, but though I have a flair for your style I seldom dig exactly what you are doing with cadences, line length, sometimes syntax, etc., and cannot handle your work as a solid object—which properties I assume you rightly claim. I don't understand the measure. I haven't worked with it much either, though, which must make the difference. But I would like to talk with you concretely on this.

I enclose these poems. The first[1] shows you where I was 2 years ago. The second, a kind of dense lyric I instinctively try to imitate[2] —after Crane, Robinson, Tate, and old Englishmen. Then the Shroudy Stranger[3] less interesting as a poem (or less sincere) but it connects observations of *things* with an old dream of the void—I have real dreams about a classic hooded figure. But this dream has become identified with my own abyss—and with the abyss of old Smokies under the Erie R.R. tracks on straight street — so the shroudy stranger[4] speaking from the inside of the old wracked bum of Paterson or anywhere in America. This is only a half made poem (using a few lines and a situation I had in a dream) . I contemplated a long work on the shroudy stranger, his wanderings. Next[5] an earlier poem, Radio City, a long lyric written in sickness. Then a mad song (to be sung by Groucho Marx to a Bop background) .[6] Then an old style ballad-type ghost dream poem.[7] Then, an Ode to the Setting Sun of abstract[8] ideas, written before leaving the hospital, and last an Ode to Judgment, which I just wrote, but which is unfinished.[9] What will come of all this I do not know yet.

I know this letter finds you in good health, as I saw you speak at the Museum in N.Y. this week. I ran backstage to accost you, but changed my mind, after waving at you, and ran off again.

Respectfully yours,<br>A. G.

---

1 ?
2 "The Voice of Rock"
3 "Please Open the Window and Let Me In"
4 "The Shrouded Stranger"
5 "Stanzas: Written at Night in Radio City"
6 "Sweet Levinsky" or "Fie My Fum"??
7 "A Dream"
8 "Ode to the Setting Sun"
9 "Ode: My 24th Year"

# THE GATES OF WRATH: 1948-1952

# TWO SONNETS

## I

I dwelled in Hell on earth to write this rhyme,
I live in stillness now, in living flame;
I witness Heaven in unholy time,
I room in the renownèd city, am
Unknown. The fame I dwell in is not mine,
I would not have it. Angels in the air
Serenade my senses in delight.
Intelligence of poets, saints and fair
Characters converse with me all night.
But all the streets are burning everywhere.
The city is burning these multitudes that climb
Her buildings. Their inferno is the same
I scaled as a stupendous blazing stair.
They vanish as I look into the light.

## II

Woe unto thee, Manhatten, woe to thee,
Woe unto all the cities of the world.
Repent, Chicagos, O repent; ah, me!
Los Angeles, now thou art gone so wild,
I think thou art still mighty, yet shall be,
As the earth shook, and San Francisco fell,
An angel in an agony of flame.
City of horrors, New York so much like Hell,
How soon thou shalt be city-without-name,
A tomb of souls, and a poor broken knell.
Fire and fire on London, Moscow shall die,
And Paris her livid atomies be rolled
Together into the Woe of the blazing bell —
All cities then shall toll for their great fame.

*1948*

# THE EYE ALTERING ALTERS ALL

Many seek and never see,
anyone can tell them why.
O they weep and O they cry
and never take until they try
unless they try it in their sleep
and never some until they die.
I ask many, they ask me.
This is a great mystery.

*East Harlem, summer 1948*

# ON READING WILLIAM BLAKE'S "THE SICK ROSE"

Rose of spirit, rose of light,
Flower whereof all will tell,
Is this black vision of my sight
The fashion of a prideful spell,
Mystic charm or magic bright,
O Judgement of fire and of fright?

What everlasting force confounded
In its being, like some human
Spirit shrunken in a bounded
Immortality, what Blossom
Inward gathers us, astounded?
Is this the sickness that is Doom?

*East Harlem, summer 1948*

# A VERY DOVE

A very Dove will have her love
    ere the Dove has died;
the spirit, vanity approve,
    will even love in pride;

and cannot love, and yet can hate,
    spirit to fulfill;
the spirit cannot watch and wait,
    the Hawk must have his kill.

There is a Gull that rolls alone
    over billows loud;
the Nightingale at night will moan
    under her soft shroud.

*East Harlem, summer 1948*

# VISION 1948

Dread spirit in me that I ever try
      With written words to move,
  Hear thou my plea, at last reply
      To my impotent pen:
  Should I endure, and never prove
      Yourself and me in love,
Tell me, spirit, tell me, O what then?

And if not love, why, then, another passion
      For me to pass in image:
  Shadow, shadow, and blind vision.
      Dumb roar of the white trance,
  Ecstatic shadow out of rage,
      Power out of passage.
Dance, dance, spirit, spirit, dance!

Is it my fancy that the world is still,
      So gentle in her dream?
  Outside, great Harlems of the will
      Move under black sleep:
  Yet in spiritual scream,
      The saxophones the same
As me in madness call thee from the deep.

I shudder with intelligence and I
      Wake in the deep light
  And hear a vast machinery
      Descending without sound,
  Intolerable to me, too bright,
      And shaken in the sight
The eye goes blind before the world goes round.

*East Harlem, summer 1948*

# DO WE UNDERSTAND EACH OTHER?

My love has come to ride me home
To our room and bed.
I had walked the wide sea path,
For my love would roam
In absence long and glad
All through our land of wrath.
We wandered wondrously,
I, still mild, true and sad,
But merry, mad and free
My love was. Look! yet come love hath.
Is this not great gentility?

I only remembered the ocean's roll,
And islands that I passed,
And, in a vision of death and dread,
A city where my soul
Visited its vast
Passage of the dead.
My love's eternity
I never entered, when, at last
"I blush with love for thee,"
My love, renewed in anger, said.
Is this not great gentility?

Over the road in an automobile
Rode I and my gentle love.
The traffic on our way was wild;
My love was at the wheel,
And in and out we drove.
My own eyes were mild.
How my love merrily
Dared the other cars to rove:
"But if they stop for me,
Why, then, I stop for them, my child."
Is this not great gentility?

*East Harlem, 1948*

8

# THE VOICE OF ROCK

I cannot sleep, I cannot sleep
until a victim is resigned;
a shadow holds me in his keep
and seeks the bones that he must find;
and hovelled in a shroudy heap
dead eyes see, and dead eyes weep,
dead men from the coffin creep,
nightmare of murder in the mind.

Murder has the ghost of shame
that lies abed with me in dirt
and mouthes the matter of my fame.
With voice of rock, and rock engirt,
a shadow cries out in my name;
he struggles for my writhing frame;
my death and his were not the same,
what wounds have I that he is hurt?

This is such murder that my own
incorporeal blood is shed,
but shadow changes into bone,
and thoughts are doubled in my head;
for what he knows and I have known
is, like a crystal lost in stone,
hidden in skin and buried down
blind as the vision of the dead.

*Paterson, 1948*

# REFRAIN

The air is dark, the night is sad,
I lie sleepless and I groan.
Nobody cares when a man goes mad:
He is sorry, God is glad.
Shadow changes into bone.

Every shadow has a name;
When I think of mine I moan,
I hear rumors of such fame.
Not for pride, but only shame,
Shadow changes into bone.

When I blush I weep for joy,
And laughter drops from me like stone:
The aging laughter of the boy
To see the ageless dead so coy.
Shadow changes into bone.

*1948*

# A WESTERN BALLAD

When I died, love, when I died
my heart was broken in your care;
I never suffered love so fair
as now I suffer and abide
when I died, love, when I died.

When I died, love, when I died
I wearied in an endless maze
that men have walked for centuries,
as endless as the gate was wide
when I died, love, when I died.

When I died, love, when I died
there was a war in the upper air:
all that happens, happens there;
there was an angel at my side
when I died, love, when I died.

*1948*

# A Western Ballad

When I died Love when I died
my heart was bro-ken in your care,
I ne-ver suf-fered love so fair
as now I suf-fer and a-bide
When I died Love when I died
When I died Love when I died
I wear-ied in an end-less maze,
that men have walked for cen-tu-ries
as end-less as the gate was wide

# SWEET LEVINSKY*

Sweet Levinsky in the night
Sweet Levinsky in the light
do you giggle out of spite,
or are you laughing in delight
sweet Levinsky, sweet Levinsky?

Sweet Levinsky, do you tremble
when the cock crows, and dissemble
as you amble to the gambol?
Why so humble when you stumble
sweet Levinsky, sweet Levinsky?

Sweet Levinsky, why so tearful,
sweet Levinsky don't be fearful,
sweet Levinsky here's your earful
of the angels chirping cheerful-
ly Levinsky, sweet Levinsky.
sweet Levinsky, sweet Levinsky.

*1949*

*Leon Levinsky is a character in Jack Kerouac's
*The Town & the City.*

14

## A MAD GLEAM

Go back to Egypt and the Greeks,
Where the Wizard understood
The spectre haunted where man seeks
And spoke to ghosts that stood in blood.

Go back, go back to the old legend;
The soul remembers, and is true:
What has been most and least imagined,
No other, there is nothing new.

The giant Phantom is ascending
Toward its coronation, gowned
With unheard music, yet unending:
Follow the flower to the ground.

*January 1949*

## PSALM

Ah, still Lord, ah, sweet Divinity
Incarnate in our grave and holy substance,
Circumscribed in this hexed endless world
Of Time, that turns a triple face, from Hell,
Imprisoned joy's incognizable thought,
To mounted earth, that shudders to conceive,
Toward angels, borne unseen out of this world,
Translate the speechless stanzas of the rose
Into my poem, and I vow to copy
Every petal on a page; perfume
My mind, ungardened, and in weedy earth;
Let these dark leaves be lit wtih images
That strike like lightning from eternal mind,
Truths that are not visible in any light
That changes and is Time, like flesh or theory,
Corruptible like any clock of meat
That sickens and runs down to die
With all those structures and machinery
Whose bones and bridges break and wash to sea
And are dissolved into green salt and coral.

A Bird of Paradise, the Nightingale
I cried for not so long ago, the poet's
Phoenix, and the erotic Swan
Which descended and transfigured Time,
And all but destroyed it, in the Dove
I speak of now, is here, I saw it here,
The Miracle, which no man knows entire,
Nor I myself. But shadow is my prophet,
I cast a shadow that surpasses me,
And I write, shadow changes into bone,
To say that still Word, the prophetic image
Beyond our present strength of flesh to bear,
Incarnate in the rain as in the sea,
Watches after us out of our eyes.
What a sweet dream! to be some incorruptible

Divinity, corporeal without a name,
Suffering metamorphosis of flesh.

Holy are the Visions of the soul
The visible mind seeks out for marriage,
As if the sleeping heart, agaze, in darkness,
Would dream her passions out as in the Heavens.
In flesh and flesh, imperfect spirits join
Vision upon vision, image upon image,
All physical and perishing, till spirit
Driven mad by Time, a ghost still haunted
By his mortal house, goes from the tomb
And drops his body back into the dirt.
I fear it till my soul remembers Heaven.
My name is Angel and my eyes are Fire!
O wonder, and more than wonder, in the world!
Now I have built my Love a sepulcher
Of whitened thoughts, and sat a year in ash,
Grieving for the lost entempled dead,
And Him who appeared to these dead eyes,
And Him my wakened beating mind remembered,
And Love that moved in substance clear as bone,
With beautiful music, at the fatal moment,
And clock stopped by its own, or hidden, hand.
These are the hollow echoes of His word.

Ah, but to have seen the Dove of still
Divinity come down in silken light of summer sun
In ignorance of the body and bone's madness.
Light falls and I fail! My youth is ending,
All my youth, and Death and Beauty cry
Like horns and motors from a ship afar,
Half heard, an echo in the sea beneath,
And Death and Beauty beckon in the dawn,
A presage of the world of whitening shadows
As another pale memorial.
Ah! but to have seen the Dove, and then go blind.

I will grow old a grey and groaning man,
Hour after hour, with each hour a thought,

And with each thought the same denial. Am I to spend
My life in praise of the idea of God?
Time leaves no hope, and leaves us none of love;
We creep and wait, we wait and go alone.
When will the heart be weary of its own
Indignity? Or Time endured destroy
The last such thoughts as these, the thoughts of Dove?
Must ravenous reason not be self consumed?
Our souls are purified of Time by Time,
And ignorance consumes itself like flesh.

Bigger and bigger gates, Thou givest, Lord,
And vaster deaths, and deaths not by my hand,
Till, in each season, as the garden dies,
I die with each, until I die no more
Time's many deaths, and pass toward the last gates,
Till come, pure light, at last to pass through pearl.
Take me to thy mansion, for I house
In clay, in a sad dolor out of joy.

Behold thy myth incarnate in my flesh
Now made incarnate in Thy Psalm, O Lord.

*1949*

# COMPLAINT OF THE SKELETON TO TIME

Take my love, it is not true,
So let it tempt no body new;
Take my lady, she will sigh
For my bed where'er I lie;
Take them, said the skeleton,
    But leave my bones alone.

Take my raiment, now grown cold,
To give to some poor poet old;
Take the skin that hoods this truth
If his age would wear my youth;
Take them, said the skeleton,
    But leave my bones alone.

Take the thoughts that like the wind
Blow my body out of mind;
Take this heart to go with that
And pass it on from rat to rat;
Take them, said the skeleton,
    But leave my bones alone.

Take the art which I bemoan
In a poem's crazy tone;
Grind me down, though I may groan,
To the starkest stick and stone;
Take them, said the skeleton,
    But leave my bones alone.

*1949*

# STANZAS: WRITTEN AT NIGHT IN RADIO CITY

If money made the mind more sane,
Or money mellowed in the bowel
The hunger beyond hunger's pain,
Or money choked the mortal growl
And made the groaner grin again,
Or did the laughing lamb embolden
To loll where has the lion lain,
I'd go make money and be golden.

Nor sex will salve the sickened soul,
Which has its holy goal an hour,
Holds to heart the golden pole,
But cannot save the silver shower,
Nor heal the sorry parts to whole.
Love is creeping under cover,
Where it hides its sleepy dole,
Else I were like any lover.

Many souls get lost at sea,
Others slave upon a stone:
Engines are not eyes to me,
Inside buildings I see bone.
Some from city to city flee,
Famous labors make them lie;
I cheat on that machinery,
Down in Arden I will die.

Art is short, nor style is sure:
Though words our virgin thoughts betray,
Time ravishes that thought most pure,
Which those who know, know anyway;
For if our daughter should endure,
When once we can no more complain,
Men take our beauty for a whore,
And like a whore, to entertain.

The city's hipper slickers shine,
Up in the attic with the bats;
The higher Chinamen, supine,
Wear a dragon in their hats:
He who seeks a secret sign
In a daze or sicker doze
Blows the flower superfine;
Not a poppy is a rose.

If fame were not a fickle charm,
There were far more famous men:
May boys amaze the world to arm,
Yet their charms are changed again,
And fearful heroes turn to harm;
But the shambles is a sham.
A few angels on a farm
Fare more fancy with their lamb.

No more of this too pretty talk,
Dead glimpses of apocalypse:
The child pissing off the rock,
Or woman withered in the lips,
Contemplate the unseen Cock
That crows all beasts to ecstasy;
And so the Saints beyond the clock
Cry to men their dead eyes see.

Come, incomparable crown,
Love my love is lost to claim,
O hollow fame that makes me groan;
We are a king without a name:
Regain thine angel's lost renown,
As, in the mind's forgotten meadow,
Where brightest shades are gazed in stone,
Man runs after his own shadow.

*1949*

# PLEASE OPEN THE WINDOW AND LET ME IN

Who is the shroudy stranger of the night,
Whose brow is mouldering green, whose reddened eye
Hides near the window trellis in dim light,
And gapes at old men, and makes children cry?

Who is the laughing walker of the street,
The alley mummy, stinking of the bone,
To dance unfixed, though bound in shadow feet,
Behind the child that creeps on legs of stone?

Who is the hungry mocker of the maze,
And haggard gate-ghost, hanging by the door,
The double mummer in whose hooded gaze
World has beckoned unto world once more?

*1949*

# THE SHROUDED STRANGER

Bare skin is my wrinkled sack
When hot Apollo humps my back
When Jack Frost grabs me in these rags
I wrap my legs with burlap bags

My flesh is cinder my face is snow
I walk the railroad to and fro
When city streets are black and dead
The railroad embankment is my bed

I sup my soup from old tin cans
And take my sweets from little hands
In Tiger Alley near the jail
I steal away from the garbage pail

In darkest night where none can see
Down in the bowels of the factory
I sneak barefoot upon stone
Come and hear the old man groan

I hide and wait like a naked child
Under the bridge my heart goes wild
I scream at a fire on the river bank
I give my body to an old gas tank

I dream that I have burning hair
Boiled arms that claw the air
The torso of an iron king
And on my back a broken wing

Who'll go out whoring into the night
On the eyeless road in the skinny moonlight
Maid or dowd or athlete proud
May wanton with me in the shroud

Who'll come lay down in the dark with me
Belly to belly and knee to knee
Who'll look into my hooded eye
Who'll lay down under my darkened thigh?

*1949*

## BOP LYRICS

When I think of death
   I get a goofy feeling;
Then I catch my breath:
   Zero is appealing,
      Appearances are hazy.
      Smart went crazy,
      Smart went crazy.

•

A flower in my head
   Has fallen through my eye;
Someday I'll be dead:
   I love the Lord on high,
      I wish He'd pull my daisy.
      Smart went crazy,
      Smart went crazy.

•

I asked the lady what's a rose,
   She kicked me out of bed.
I asked the man, and so it goes,
   He hit me on the head.
      Nobody knows,
      Nobody knows,
   At least nobody's said.

•

The time I went to China
To lead the boy scout troops,
They sank my ocean liner,
And all I said was "Oops!"

•

All the doctors think I'm crazy;
The truth is really that I'm lazy:
I made visions to beguile 'em
Till they put me in th'asylum

●

I'm a pot and God's a potter,
And my head's a piece of putty.
    Ark my darkness,
    Lark my looks,
I'm so lucky to be nutty.

*1949*

# FIE MY FUM

Pull my daisy,
Tip my cup,
Cut my thoughts
For coconuts,

Bone my shadow,
Dove my soul,
Set a halo
On my skull,

Ark my darkness,
Rack my lacks,
Bleak my lurking,
Lark my looks,

Start my Arden,
Gate my shades,
Silk my garden,
Rose my days,

Whore my door,
Stone my dream,
Milk my mind
And make me cream,

Say my oops,
Ope my shell,
Roll my bones,
Ring my bell,

Pope my parts,
Pop my pot,
Poke my pap,
Pit my plum.

*1949*

## PULL MY DAISY

Pull my daisy
tip my cup
all my doors are open
Cut my thoughts
for coconuts
all my eggs are broken
Jack my Arden
gate my shades
woe my road is spoken
Silk my garden
rose my days
now my prayers awaken

Bone my shadow
dove my dream
start my halo bleeding
Milk my mind &
make me cream
drink me when you're ready
Hop my heart on
harp my height
seraphs hold me steady
Hip my angel
hype my light
lay it on the needy

Heal the raindrop
sow the eye
bust my dust again
Woe the worm
work the wise
dig my spade the same
Stop the hoax
what's the hex
where's the wake
how's the hicks
take my golden beam

Rob my locker
lick my rocks
leap my cock in school
Rack my lacks
lark my looks
jump right up my hole
Whore my door
beat my boor
eat my snake of fool
Craze my hair
bare my poor
asshole shorn of wool

Say my oops
ope my shell
bite my naked nut
Roll my bones
ring my bell
call my worm to sup
Pope my parts
pop my pot
raise my daisy up
Poke my pap
pit my plum
let my gap be shut

*— Allen Ginsberg, Jack Kerouac & Neal Cassady*

## SOMETIME JAILHOUSE BLUES

Sometime I'll lay down my wrath,
As I lay my body down
Between the ache of breath and breath,
Golden slumber in the bone.

Thought's a stone, though sweet or sorry,
Run-down from an uphill climb:
Money, money, work and worry,
And all the aimless toil of Time.

Sometime I look up in light
And see the weary sun go West;
Sometime I see the moon at night
Go hidden in her cloudy rest.

Sometime tears of death will blind
All that was worldly, wise or fair,
And visioned by the death of mind
My ghost will wander in the air,

And gaze upon a ghostly face,
Not knowing what was fair or lost,
Remembering not what flesh lay waste,
Or made him kind as ghost to ghost.

*1949*

## AN EASTERN BALLAD

I speak of love that comes to mind:
The moon is faithful, although blind;
She moves in thought she cannot speak.
Perfect care has made her bleak.

I never dreamed the sea so deep,
The earth so dark; so long my sleep,
I have become another child.
I wake to see the world go wild.

*1945-49*

# EPIGRAM ON A PAINTING OF GOLGOTHA

On a bare tree in a hollow place,
A blinded form's unhaloed face;
Sight, where Heaven is destroyed,
The hanging visage of the void.

*1949-50*

# A DREAM

I waked at midmost in the night,
Dim lamp shuddering in the bell,
House enwracked with natal light
That glowed as in a ghostly shell.

I rose and darked the hornlike flare,
And watched the shadows in the room
Crawl on walls and empty air
Through the window from the moon.

I stared in phantom-attic dark
At such radiant shapes of gloom,
I thought my fancy and mind's lark
So cried for Death that He had come.

As sleepy faced night walkers go,
Room to room, and down the stair,
Through the labyrinth to and fro,
So I paced sleepless in nightmare.

I walked out to the city tower,
Where, as in a stony cell,
Time lay prisoned, and twelfth hour
Complained upon the midnight bell.

I met a boy on the city street,
Fair was his hair, and fair his eyes,
Walking in his winding sheet,
As fair as was my own disguise.

He walked his way in a white shroud,
His cheek was whiter than his gown.
He looked at me, and spoke aloud,
And all his voice was but a groan:

"My love is dreaming of me now,
For I have dreamed him oft so well

That in my ghostly sleep I go
To find him by the midnight bell.

And so I walk and speak these lines
Which he will hear and understand.
If some poor wandering child of time
Finds me, let him take my hand,

And I will lead him to the stone,
And I will lead him through the grave,
But let him fear no light of bone,
And let him fear no dark of wave,

And we will walk the double door
That breaks upon the ageless night,
Where I have come, and must once more
Return, and so forsake the light."

The darkness that is half disguised
In the Zodiac of my dream
Gazed on me in his bleak eyes,
And I became what now I seem.

Once my crown was silk and black;
I have dreamed, and I awake.
Now that time has wormed my cheek,
Horns and willows me bespeak.

*Paterson, December 1949*

# ODE TO THE SETTING SUN*

*The Jersey Marshes in rain, November evening, seen from Susquehanna Railroad*

The wrathful East of smoke and iron
Crowded in a broken crown;
The Archer of the Jersey mire
Naked in a rusty gown;
Railroad creeping toward the fire
Where the carnal sun goes down.

Apollo's shining chariot's shadow
Shudders in the mortal bourn;
Amber shores upon the meadow
Where Phaëthon falls forlorn
Fade in somber chiaroscuro,
Phantoms of the burning morn.

Westward to the world's blind gaze,
In funeral of raining cloud,
The motionless cold Heavens blaze,
Born out of a dying crowd;
Daybreak in the end of days,
Bloody light beneath the shroud.

In vault dominion of the night
The hosts of prophecy convene,
Till, empire of the lark alight,
Their bodies waken as we dream,
And put our raiment on, and bright
Crown, still haloed though unseen.

Under the earth there is an eye
Open in a sightless cave,
And the skull in Eternity
Bares indifference to the grave:
Earth turns, and the day must die,
And the sea accepts the wave.

My bones are carried on the train
Westward where the sun has gone;
Night has darkened in the rain,
And the rainbow day is done;
Cities age upon the plain
And smoke rolls upward out of stone.

*1949-1950*

*See "Sunset" in *Empty Mirror*.

## CRASH

There is more to Fury
Than men imagine,
Who drive a pallid jury
On a pale engine.

In a spinning plane,
A false machine,
The pilot drops in flame
From the unseen.

*1950*

## AN IMAGINARY ROSE IN A BOOK

Oh dry old rose of God,
that with such bleak perfume
changed images to blood
and body to a tomb,

what fragrance you have lost,
and are now withered mere
crimson myth of dust
and recollection sere

of an unfading garden
whereof the myriad life
and all that flock in blossom,
none other met the knife.

*1950*

# IN MEMORIAM

*William Cannestra 1922-1950*


He cast off all his golden robes
and lay down sleeping in the night,
and in a dream he saw three fates
at a machine in a shroud of light.

He yelled "I wait the end of Time;
be with me, shroud, now, in my wrath!
There is a lantern in my grave,
who hath that lantern all light hath."

Alas! The prophet of this dream
is sunken in the dumbing clime:
much is finished, much forgotten
in the wrack and wild love of time.

It's death that makes man's life a dream
and heaven's splendor but a wave;
light that falls into the sea
is swallowed in a starving cave.

Skin may be visionary till the crystal
skull is coaled in aged shade,
but underground the lantern dies,
shroud must rot, and memory fade.

Who talks of Death and Angel now,
great angel darkened out of grace?
The shroud enfolds your radiant doom,
the silent Parcae change the race,

while the man of the apocalypse
shall with his wrath lay ever wed
until the sexless womb bear love,
and the grave be weary of the dead,

tragical master broken down
into a self embodied tomb,
blinded by the sight of death,
and woven in the darkened loom.

*1950*

## ODE: MY 24TH YEAR

Now I have become a man
and know no more than mankind can
and groan with nature's every groan,
transcending child's blind skeleton
and all childish divinity,
while loomed in consanguinity
the weaving of the shroud goes on.

No two things alike; and yet
first memory dies, then I forget
one carnal thought that made thought grim:
but that has sunk below time's rim
and wonder ageing into woe
later dayes more fatal show:
Time gets thicker, light gets dim.

And I a second Time am blind,
all starlight dimmed out of the mind
that was first candle to the morn,
and candelabra turned to thorn.
All is dream till morn has rayed
the Rose of night back into shade,
Messiah firmament reborn.

Now I cannot go be wild
or harken back to shape of child
chrystal born into the aire
circled by the harte and bear
and agelesse in a greene arcade,
for he is down in Granite laid,
or standing on a Granite stair.

No return, where thought's completed;
let that ghost's last gaze go cheated:
I may waste my days no more
pining in spirituall warre.

Where am I in wilderness?
What creature bore my bones to this?
Here is no Eden: this is my store.

*1950-1951, unfinished*

EARLIER POEMS: 1947

*To Neal Cassady*

# A FURTHER PROPOSAL

Come live with me and be my love,
And we will some old pleasures prove.
Men like me have paid in verse
This costly courtesy, or curse;

But I would bargain with my art,
(As to the mind, now to the heart)
My symbols, images, and signs
Please me more outside these lines.

For your share and recompense,
You will be taught another sense:
The wisdom of the subtle worm
Will turn most perfect in your form.

Not that your soul need tutored be
By intellectual decree,
But graces that the mind can share
Will make you, as more wise, more fair,

Till all the world's devoted thought
Find all in you it ever sought,
And even I, of skeptic mind,
A Resurrection of a kind.

This compliment, in my own way,
For what I would receive, I pay;
Thus all the wise have writ thereof,
And all the fair have been their love.

*1947*

# A LOVER'S GARDEN

How vainly lovers marvel, all
To make a body, mind, and soul,
Who, winning one white night of grace,
Will weep and rage a year of days,
Or muse forever on a kiss,
If won by a more sad mistress —
Are all these lovers, then, undone
By him and me, who love alone?

O, have the virtues of the mind
Been all for this one love designed?
As seconds on the clock do move,
Each marks another thought of love;
Thought follows thought, and we devise
Each minute to antithesize,
Till, as the hour chimes its tune,
Dialectic, we commune.

The argument our minds create
We do, abed, substantiate;
Nor we disdain, in our delight,
To flatter the old Stagirite:
For in one speedy moment, we
Endure the whole Eternity,
And in our darkened shapes have found
The greater world that we surround.

In this community, the soul
Doth make its act impersonal,
As, locked in a mechanic bliss,
It shudders into nothingness —
Three characters of each may die
To dramatize that Unity.
Timed, placed, and acting thus, the while,
We sit and sing, and sing and smile.

What life is this? What pleasure mine!
Such as no image can insign:

Nor sweet music, understood,
Soft at night, in solitude
At a window, will enwreathe
Such stillness on my brow: I breathe,
And walk on earth, and act my will,
And cry Peace! Peace! and all is still.

Though here, it seems, I must remain,
My thoughtless world, whereon men strain
Through lives of motion without sense,
Farewell! in this benevolence —
That all men may, as I, arrange
A love as simple, sweet, and strange
As few men know; nor can I tell,
But only imitate farewell.

*1947*

# LOVE LETTER

Let not the sad perplexity
Of absent love unhumor thee:
Sighs, tears, and oaths, and laughter I have spent
To make my play with thee resolve in merriment;
For wisest critics past agree
The truest love is comedy.
Will thou not weary of the tragic argument?

Would'st thou make love perverse, and then
Preposterous and crabbed, my pen?
Tempt Eros not (he is more wise than I)
To suck the apple of thy sad absurdity.
Love, who is a friend to men,
You'ld make a Devil of again:
Then should I be once more exiled, alas, in thee.

Make peace with me, and in my kind,
With Eros, angel of the mind,
Who loves me, loving thee, and in our bliss
Is loved by all of us and finds his happiness.
Such simple pleasures are designed
To entertain our days, I find,
And so shalt thee, when next we make a night of this.

This spring we'll be not merely mad,
But absent lovers, therefore sad,
So we'll be no more happy than we ought —
That simple love of Eros may be strangely taught.
And wit will seldom make me glad
That spring hath not what winter had,
Therefore these nights are darkened shadows of my thought.

Grieve in a garden, then, and in a summer's twilight,
Think of thy love, for spring is lost to me.
Or as you will, and if the moon be white,
Let all thy soul to music married be,
To magic, nightingales, and immortality;

And, if it pleases thee, why, think on Death;
For Death is strange upon a summer night,
The thought of it may make thee catch thy breath,
And meditation hath itself a great beauty;
Wherefore if thou must weep, now I must mourn with thee.

*Easter Sunday, 1947*

## DAKAR DOLDRUMS

### I

Most dear, and dearest at this moment most,
Since this my love for thee is thus more free
Than that I cherished more dear and lost;
Most near, now nearest where I fly from thee:
Thy love most consummated is in absence,
Half for the trust I have for thee in mind,
Half for the pleasures of thee in remembrance —
Thou art most full and fair of all thy kind.

Not half so fair as thee is fate I fear,
Wherefore my sad departure from this season
Wherein for some love of me thou held'st me dear,
While I betray thee for a better reason.
I am a brutish agonist, I know
Lust or its consummation cannot ease
These miseries of mind, this mask like sorrow:
It is myself, not thee, shall make my peace.

Yet, O sweet soul, to have possessed thy love,
The meditations of thy mind for me,
Hath half deceived a thought that ill shall prove.
It was a grace of fate, this scene of comedy
Foretold more tragic acts in my short age.
Yet 'tis no masque of mine, no mere sad play
Spectacular upon an empty stage —
My life is more unreal, another way.

To lie with thee, to touch thee with desire,
Enrage the summer nights with thy mere presence —
Flesh hath such joy, such sweetness, and such fire!
The white ghost fell on me, departing thence.
Henceforth I must perform a winter mood;
Belovèd gestures freeze in bitter ice,
Eyes glare through a pale jail of solitude,
Fear chills my mind: Here endeth all my bliss!

Cursed may be this month of Fall! I fail
My full and fair and near and dear and kind.
I but endure my role, my own seas sail,
Far from the sunny shores within thy mind.
So this departure shadoweth mine end:
Ah! what poor human cometh unto me,
Since now the snowy spectre doth descend,
Henceforth I shall in fear and anger flee.


II

Lord, forgive my passions, they are old,
And restive as the years that I have known.
To what abandonments have I foretold
My bondage? And have mine own love undone!
How mad my youth, my sacramental passage!
Yet I dream these September journeys true:
When five days flowed like sickness in this knowledge,
I vomited out my mockery, all I knew.


III

Five nights upon the deep I suffered presage,
Five dawns familiar seabirds cried me pale:
I care not now, for I have seen an image
In the sea that was no Nightingale.

— My love, and doth still that rare figurine
In thy sad garden sing, now I am gone?
Sweet carols that I made, and caroller serene,
They broke my heart, and sang for thee alone.
Secret to thee the Nightingale was Death;
So all the figures are that I create.
For thee awhile I breathed another breath,
To make my Death thy Beauty imitate. —

More terrible than these are the vast visions
Of the sea, nor comprehensible.
Last night I stared upon the Cuban mountains,
Tragic in the mist, as on my soul,
Star studded in the dark, sea shaded round

51

And still, a funeral of Emperors,
Wind wound in ruined shrouds and crescent crowned
And tombed in desolation on dead shores.

The place was dread with age: the evening tide,
Eternal wife of death that washed these bones,
Turns back to sea by night, eternal bride:
She claspèd my ship and rocked to hear its groans.
I did imagine I had known this sea,
Had been an audience to this before;
The place was prescient, like a great stage in me,
As out of a dream that late I dream no more.

I did imagine I had known this sea;
It raged like a great beast in my passage,
Till I, enragèd creature, anciently
Engendered here, cried out upon mine image:
"How long in absence O thou journeyest,
Ages my soul and ages! Here ever home
In this sea's endangerments thou sufferest;
And do, and do, and now my will hath done!"

Ah, love, I tell thee true, nor false affix
The solitude I watched by th'iron prow:
While I interpreted I stared me sick
At transformations in the tides below;
For the grim bride rose up, and all surrounding,
Carried me through the star-piercèd air,
Till I cried Stay! and Stay! surrendering
My movèd soul in flight to faster fear.

As I dived then I cried, delving all depthed in foam,
"Now close in weeds thy wave-lipped womb, mistress!"
But she ope'd her watering wounds and drew me down
And drove me dancing through the white-wreathed darkness.
Though I stood still to memorize the deep,
And woke my eyes wild-wide upon the height,
My soul it feareth its descent to keep,
My soul it turneth in its famous flight.

## IV

Ha! now I die or no, I fear this tide
Carrieth me still, perishing, past where I stood,
So mild, to gaze whereat I long had died,
Or shall, as well, in future solitude.
What other shores are there I still remember?
I was in a pale land, I looked through a pure vision
In a pallid dawn, with a half vacant glare.
Alas! what harbour hath the imagination?

O the transparent past hath a white port,
Tinted in the eye; it doth appear
Sometime on dark days, much by night, to sport
Bright shades like dimes of silver shining there,
On red dull sands on green volcanic shores.
I thought these stanzas out this cloudy noon,
Past Cuba now, past Haiti's stony jaws,
In the last passage to Dakar. The moon

Alone was full as it had been all year,
Orange and strange at dawn. It was my eyes,
Not Africa, did this: they shined so pure
Each island floated by a sweet surprise.
Coins, then, on Cape Verdi's peakèd cones
Sparkle out with pallors various.
It makes me God to pass these mortal towns:
Real people sicken here upon slopes sulphurous.

So in my years I saw my serious cities
Colored with Love and chiming with Nightingales,
Architectural with fantasies,
With fools in schools and geniuses in jails.
When in sweet vivid dreams such rainbows rise,
and spectral children dance among the music,
I watch them still: hot emeralds are their eyes!
My eyes are ice, alas! How white I wake!

# V

Twenty days have drifted in the wake
Of this slow agèd ship that carries coal
From Texas to Dakar. I, for the sake
Of little but my causelessness of soul,
Am carried out of my chill hemisphere
To unfamiliar summer on the earth.
I spend my days to meditate a fear;
Each day I give the sea is one of death.

This is the last night of the outward journeying,
The darkness falleth westward unto thee;
And I must end my labors of this evening,
And all the last long night, and all this day:
It doth give peace, thus to torment the soul,
Till it is sundered from its forms and sense,
Till it surrendereth its knowledge whole,
And stares on the world out of a sleepless trance.

So on these stanzas doth a peace descend,
Now I have journeyed through these images
To come upon no image in the end.
So are we consummated in these passages,
Most near and dear and far apart in fate.
As I mean no mere sweet philosophy,
So I, unto a world I must create,
Turn with no promise and no prophecy.

*South Atlantic, 1947*

# HINDSIGHT

*Gates of Wrath's* first sonnets, "Woe to Thee Manhattan," were in-
spired by first reading ms. of Kerouac's triumphant record of youth
family *The Town and the City*. All poems hermetic "The Eye
Altering" thru "A Western Ballad" refer to breakthru of visionary
consciousness 1948 described elsewhere prosaically: early mind-
manifesting flashes catalyzed by lonely despair I felt at sudden ter-
mination of erotic spiritual marriage mutually vowed by myself and
Neal Cassady. The "Earlier Poems," 1947, were love poems to N.C.,
though love's gender was kept closet. "Sweet Levinsky" (counter-
image to Kerouac's tender caricature) thru "Pull My Daisy" were
written Jack much in mind ear. "Pull My Daisy" 's form grew out of
J.K.'s adaptation of "Smart Went Crazy" refrain: recombining
images jazzier as

> Pull my daisy,
> Tip my cup,
> All my doors are open —

from my more wooden verse.
Jack brought this verse into York Ave. coldwater flat — I remember
his athletic pencil-dash'd handscript, notebooked. I replicated that
form and Jack dubbed in more lines — about a third of the poem
was his. One line "How's the Hicks?" was tossed to us as we walked
into Cassady's midnite NY parkinglot 1949 asking Neal "What's the
Hex, Who's the Hoax?"

"Sometime Jailhouse" poems to "Ode 24th Year" reflect early
dope-type bust & subsequent hospital rehabilitation solitude-bench
dolmen realms so characteristic of mental penology late 40s con-
temporary. The letter to W.C.W. enclosing poems was answered
thus: "In this mode perfection is basic." The poems were imperfect.
I responded by sending Williams several speedworthy notations that
form the basis of book *Empty Mirror*, texts written roughly same
years as these imperfect lyrics.

*Gates of Wrath* ms. was carried to London by lady friend early fifties, it disappeared, and I had no complete copy till 1968 when old typescript was returned thru poet Bob Dylan—it passed into his hands years earlier. By sweet coincidence, I returned to this rhymed mode with Dylan's encouragement as fitted for musical song. Tuned to lyric guitar, composing on harmonium, chant or improvising on rhythmic chords in electric studio, I began 'perfecting' use of this mode two decades after W.C.W.'s wise objection, dear reader, in same weeks signatur'd below.

ALLEN GINSBERG
*December 8, 1971*

# DATE DUE

| OCT 04 2001 | | | |
|---|---|---|---|
| | | | |
| | | | |
| | | | |
| | | | |
| | | | |
| | | | |
| | | | |
| | | | |
| | | | |
| | | | |
| | | | |
| | | | |
| | | | |
| | | | |
| | | | |
| | | | |
| | | | |